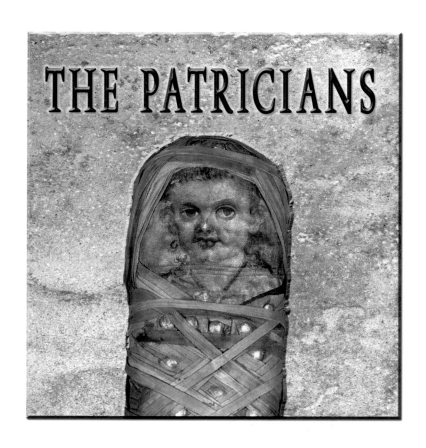

THE PATRICIANS

LIFE IN THE ROMAN EMPIRE

THE PATRICIANS

BY

KATHRYN HINDS

BENCHMARK BOOKS

MARSHALL CAVENDISH
NEW YORK

Once again, to the Lumpkin Library Ladies—
sine qua non

The author and publisher wish to specially thank J. Brett McClain
of the Oriental Institute of the University of Chicago
for his invaluable help in reading the manuscript.

❦

Benchmark Books   Marshall Cavendish   99 White Plains Road   Tarrytown, New York 10591-9001
www.marshallcavendish.com   Copyright © 2005 by Marshall Cavendish Corporation   All rights
reserved. No part of this book may be reproduced or utilized in any form or by any means electronic
or mechanical including photocopying, recording, or by any information storage and retrieval
system, without permission from the copyright holders.   All Internet sites were available and accurate when this book was sent to press.   Book design by Michael Nelson   LIBRARY OF CONGRESS
CATALOGING-IN-PUBLICATION DATA: Hinds, Kathryn, 1962-   The Patricians / by Kathryn Hinds.
p. cm. — (Life in the Roman empire)   Includes bibliographical references and index.   ISBN 0-7614-1654-4
1. Patricians (Rome)—Juvenile literature. 2. Social classes—Rome—Juvenile literature. 3. Rome—
Social life and customs—Juvenile literature. 4.   Rome—History—30 B.C.-284 A.D.—Juvenile
literature. I. Title II. Series: Hinds, Kathryn, 1962- . Life in the Roman empire.   DG83.3.H55
2004   937'.07'08621—dc22   2004003080

Art Research: Rose Corbett Gordon, Mystic CT
Photo Credits: Front cover: Metropolitan Museum of Art, New York/Bridgeman Art Library Back
cover: Scala/Art Resource, NY   Pages i, viii, 5 left, 11, 25, 29, 49, 52: Erich Lessing/Art Resource, NY;
pages iii, 6, 19, 21: Scala/Art Resource, NY; page vi: Nimatallah/Art Resource, NY; pages 3, 9 right: Louvre, Paris/Giraudon/Bridgeman Art Library; page 5 right: Private Collection/Bridgeman Art Library; page
9 left: SEF/Art Resource, NY; page 13: Vanni/Art Resource, NY; page 14: Bill Ross/Corbis; page 15: Vic-
toria Art Gallery, Bath and North East Somerset Council/Bridgeman Art Library; page 16: Archivo
Iconografico, S.A./Corbis; page 17: The Art Archive / Dagli Orti; page 18: Forum, Rome/Giraudon/Bridge-
man Art Library; page 23: Musée National du Bardo, Le Bardo/Giraudon/Bridgeman Art Library; page
24, 62: Gilles Mermet/Art Resource, NY; page 26: The Art Archive / Museo Prenestino Palestrina / Dagli
Orti; page 32: Kunsthistorisches Museum, Vienna/Bridgeman Art Library; page 34: Museum of Lon-
don/Topham/The Image Works; page 36: The Art Archive / Musée du Louvre Paris / Dagli Orti; page
39: Villa dei Misteri, Pompeii, Italy/Bridgeman Art Library; page 41: Burstein Collection/Corbis; page 42:
Museo Archeologico Nazionale, Naples, Italy/Bridgeman Art Library; page 44: The Art Archive / Archae-
ological Museum Vaison-la-Romaine / Dagli Orti;   page 47: Metropolitan Museum of Art, New
York/Bridgeman Art Library; page 50: The Art Archive / Museo della Civilta Romana Rome / Dagli Orti;
page 54: The Art Archive / Musée Lapidaire d'Art Paien Arles / Dagli Orti; page 57: The Art Archive /
Bibliotheque des Arts Decoratifs Paris / Dagli Orti.

Printed in China
1 3 5 6 4 2

front cover: Fresco of an upper-class woman relaxing, attended by a young slave
back cover: Marble relief of the imperial family during the reign of Augustus
half-title page: Funeral portrait of an upper-class child from Roman-ruled Egypt
title page: A wealthy young woman with a writing tablet and stylus
About the Roman Empire, p. vi: A portion of a mosaic showing a lively riverside party

CONTENTS

⋘⋙

⋘⋙

ABOUT THE ROMAN EMPIRE

When we think about the Roman Empire, we often picture gladiators, chariot races, togas, marble statues, and legions on the march. These images tell only part of the story of ancient Rome. According to the Romans themselves, their city was founded in 753 B.C.E.[*] At first Rome was a kingdom, then it became a republic. In 27 B.C.E. Augustus Caesar became Rome's absolute ruler—its first emperor. Meanwhile, this city built on seven hills overlooking the Tiber River had been steadily expanding its power. In Augustus's time Rome controlled all of Italy and the rest of mainland Europe west of the Rhine River and south of the Danube River, as well as much of North Africa and the Middle East.

At its height, the Roman Empire reached all the way from Britain to Persia. It brought together an array of European, African, and Middle Eastern peoples, forming a vibrant multicultural society. During much of the empire's existence, its various ethnic and religious groups got along with remarkable tolerance and understanding—a model that can still inspire us today. We can also be inspired by the Romans' tremendous achievements in the arts, architecture, literature, law, and philosophy, just as they have inspired and influenced people in Europe and the Americas for hundreds of years.

So step back in time, and visit Rome at its most powerful, from 27 B.C.E. to around 200 C.E., the first two centuries of the empire. In this book you will meet emperors, senators, generals, and poets, as well as women and children of the imperial court. These people had many of the same joys and sorrows, hopes and fears that we do, but their world was very different from ours. Forget about telephones, computers, cars, and televisions, and imagine what it might have been like to live among Rome's patricians, the ruling class who dominated much of the ancient world. Welcome to life in the Roman Empire. . . .

* A variety of systems of dating have been used by different cultures throughout history. Many historians now prefer to use B.C.E (Before Common Era) and C.E. (Common Era) instead of B.C. (Before Christ) and A.D. (Anno Domini), out of respect for the diversity of the world's peoples. In this book, all dates are C.E. unless otherwise noted.

I

THE MAN AT THE TOP

IT BECAME ESSENTIAL TO PEACE, THAT ALL POWER
SHOULD BE CENTERED IN ONE MAN.
—TACITUS, *HISTORIES*

he ancient Romans hated kings. They had learned their history lessons well: the last few kings who ruled Rome in its early days were foreigners whom later generations remembered as corrupt tyrants. After the overthrow of the royal house in 509 B.C.E., the Roman republic was set up so that no one person would be able to hold absolute power. Two consuls headed the government. They were elected for one-year terms and equally shared *imperium,* the authority to command troops and to interpret and carry out the law. The consuls also played the leading role in the Senate, the body that created new laws and handled the republic's finances and foreign relations. Senators were not elected. Once a man had served in an elected office, he automatically became a member of the Senate for life.

opposite:
Julius Caesar gained so much control over the government that many Romans were afraid he would make himself king.

Consuls and other government officials were chosen by assemblies that were open to all male Roman citizens—that is, free men who met certain other qualifications. Assemblies of male citizens also voted on whether or not to go to war and whether or not to pass the laws proposed by the Senate. When the assemblies officially met, they could not debate the issues they were deciding on. Before a vote was held, however, discussion often took place at unofficial meetings, which could also be attended by women, slaves, and foreigners.

Rome's republican government was not "of the people, by the people, and for the people" in the sense that we understand today. Only wealthy nobles—a small portion of the population—were in a position to take active part in government and politics. These people cherished their freedom from one-man rule. Yet as Rome conquered more and more of the Mediterranean world, the republic became increasingly difficult to govern efficiently. And as Rome grew more powerful and wealthy, there were Roman politicians and generals who could not resist the temptation to acquire some of that wealth and power for themselves.

In 44 B.C.E. Julius Caesar, the victor in a brutal civil war that had threatened to destroy the republic, had himself declared dictator for life. In the past, the consuls sometimes appointed a dictator to take absolute command of the army and government during an emergency—but the dictator's term only lasted six months. Caesar's move angered many senators, and a group of them murdered him—but they could not save the republic. After another fourteen years of civil war, Caesar's grandnephew and adopted son Octavian emerged victorious. In 27 B.C.E. the Senate gave him the title Augustus (meaning "revered" or "worthy of honor"), and he claimed that he had restored the republic. In reality, he alone now controlled Rome—and its empire.

IMPERIAL POWERS

Augustus, an extremely intelligent and diplomatic man, was careful not to make the mistake that had doomed Julius Caesar. Instead of proclaiming himself dictator or king, he took the title *princeps,* "first citizen." Operating within the framework that had upheld Rome for nearly five hundred years, he served as one of the two annually elected consuls. The old republican forms of government were carefully maintained. The Senate and assemblies still met, and the powers that Augustus wielded were clearly defined, not arbitrary.

The *princeps,* however, was so enormously wealthy and influential that over the course of many years he was able to acquire the powers of every important office in the Roman government. For nine years in a row Augustus was elected a consul. After this, he was given lifelong tribunician power—the power that, in the republic, had belonged to officials called tribunes— enabling him to veto any laws, elections, decrees of the Senate, or actions of other officials. The Senate also repeatedly voted Augustus control of the provinces of Egypt, Gaul (present-day France and Belgium), Spain, and Syria—the large, important provinces where most of Rome's military forces were stationed. In 12 B.C.E. he was even elected to the lifelong position of high priest of the Roman

First citizen Augustus wearing a toga, the age-old formal dress of all male Roman citizens

state religion. It is no wonder that, as the historian Dio Cassius wrote around 200 C.E., "Nothing . . . was done which did not please Augustus."

Some senators resented the new state of affairs. Most Romans, however, seemed glad to accept the rule of Augustus. People were tired of decades of civil war and were grateful to the *princeps* for bringing peace and prosperity back to Rome. They felt that the government was now far more stable and efficient, and much less corrupt, than it had been in the later years of the republic. Augustus further won the people's favor by such actions as beautifying the city of Rome, renovating its temples, improving its water supply, sponsoring free public entertainment, and lowering the price of grain. He gave land or money to all retiring soldiers, and several times distributed money from his personal funds, or grain bought with his own money, to hundreds of thousands of Roman commoners.

Augustus ruled the Roman Empire for some forty years, dying in 14 C.E. at the age of about seventy-six. He had made sure that his stepson Tiberius would succeed him as *princeps*: during Augustus's lifetime, the Senate had given Tiberius tribunician power and *imperium,* and he had successfully served in a number of military and administrative posts. As the heir of Augustus's wealth and a man experienced in public service, Tiberius was easily accepted as emperor. Strabo, a Greek historian writing during the reign of Tiberius, affirmed that "the Romans and their allies have never enjoyed such an abundance of peace and prosperity as that which Augustus Caesar provided from the time when he first assumed absolute power, and which his son and successor, Tiberius, is now providing."

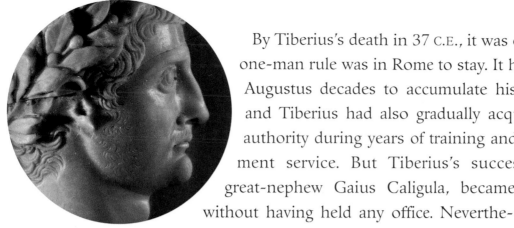

By Tiberius's death in 37 C.E., it was clear that one-man rule was in Rome to stay. It had taken Augustus decades to accumulate his powers, and Tiberius had also gradually acquired his authority during years of training and government service. But Tiberius's successor, his great-nephew Gaius Caligula, became *princeps* without having held any office. Nevertheless, the Senate voted him all the powers that had been held by Augustus and Tiberius, and so it was with the emperors who followed. The Senate and people of Rome had come to accept without question the emperors' power, in the words of Dio Cassius, "to make levies, to collect money, to declare war, to make peace, to rule foreigners and citizens alike, anytime, anywhere."

WORKING WITH THE SENATE

During Rome's centuries as a republic, the Senate had been supreme. Senators and their families made up the wealthiest and most privileged class in Roman society. Even as Augustus accumulated his powers of government, he was careful to maintain the best possible relationship with the Senate, since it represented the interests of the wealthy and influential nobility. The highest government posts were still reserved for the senators. The Senate and its members also continued to deal with routine government business in Italy and in the provinces that were not under the emperor's direct control.

Augustus and Tiberius both made important changes in the Senate's activities and procedures. Augustus tried to make the Senate a

top left:
Tiberius, the second emperor

top right:
Gaius Caligula, portrayed on a gold coin

more efficient body by decreasing its size from a thousand men to about six hundred. He also gave it a new role as a high court of law, hearing and judging cases of political importance (although some later emperors preferred to judge such cases themselves). In 5 B.C.E. Augustus set another pattern for the future by having two pairs of consuls elected every year, each pair serving a six-month term. Soon after coming to power, Tiberius did away with elections in the assemblies, which afterward met only for ceremonial purposes. From that time, all officials were elected by the Senate, and laws were passed by decrees of the Senate or edicts from the emperor.

The relationship between emperors and the Senate varied depending on circumstances and the people involved. Some emperors worked well with the Senate, while others—who were felt to seriously abuse their power—were hated by the Senate. Few senators could take the chance of standing up to the all-powerful emperor. At the same time, most emperors felt that it was wise not to offend the Senate, for they depended on senators to carry out many government functions. In any case, by the middle of the first century most senators had been nominated for office by the emperor himself. This meant that the Senate was largely filled with men loyal to the emperor (although they might not be so loyal to a succeeding emperor). The consuls and other officials had more prestige than real power. As the great Roman historian Tacitus put it, the senators had accepted the "futility of long speeches in the Senate, when the best men were quick to reach agreement elsewhere, and of endless haranguing of public meetings, when the final decisions were taken not by the ignorant multitude but by one man."

THE EMPEROR AND THE ARMY

Much of the emperor's power came from his control of the army. Early on, Augustus had taken an additional first name, *Imperator*—the source of our word "emperor"—meaning "commander in chief." (During the republic this had been a title granted to generals only temporarily, in honor of great victories.) By the seventies C.E., *Imperator* had become the usual title of the Roman ruler, highlighting his role as supreme military commander.

The imperial Roman army was made up of twenty-five to thirty-three units called legions, with around five thousand men in each. The legions were generally stationed along the empire's borders or in provinces where trouble was likely to arise. Auxiliaries—additional troops made up mostly of non-Roman citizens—supported the legions. Each legion was commanded by a legionary legate, a senator appointed by the emperor. A provincial governor—also chosen by the emperor—had military authority over all the legions stationed in his province. When there was fighting to be done in a province, it was generally the governor who took charge of the campaign as the emperor's representative.

A number of emperors led the army themselves. The emperor Trajan, for instance, waged three wars during his reign, adding to the empire Armenia, Mesopotamia, and Dacia, a large territory north of the Danube. Trajan was extremely popular with the army because he shared their dangers and hardships on campaign—and he seems to have genuinely enjoyed military life. Dio Cassius wrote, "even if he did delight in war, nevertheless he was satisfied when success had been achieved, a most bitter foe overthrown and his countrymen exalted."

Sometimes when an emperor died and it was unclear who should succeed him, the army would declare one of its generals the new emperor. The army might even oust an emperor to replace him with its own candidate. During the year 69 C.E. this happened more than once. First the legions stationed in Germany revolted against the emperor Galba and proclaimed their commander, Vitellius, emperor. Galba was assassinated shortly afterward, and soldiers in the city of Rome declared another man emperor, Otho. A brief civil war ended in the death of Otho, but Vitellius's rule was not secure. The legions in Egypt and along the Danube River supported a new claimant to the throne, Vespasian, a popular general with an impressive service record. By the end of 69, Vespasian's forces were in control of Rome. Vespasian proved himself worthy of the army's faith in him, ruling the empire justly and wisely for ten years. The events of the year 69, however, proved an important point. Just as emperors controlled the Senate but also needed its support, so it was with the army: an emperor who did not have the army behind him was unlikely to stay in power for long.

⊃ THE FIRST TWENTY-ONE EMPERORS ⊂

Augustus, 27 B.C.E.–14 C.E.

Tiberius, 14–37

Gaius Caligula, 37–41

Claudius, 41–54

Nero, 54–68

Galba, 68–69

Otho, 69

Vitellius, 69

Vespasian, 69–79

Titus, 79–81

Domitian, 81–96

Nerva, 96–98

Trajan, 98–117

Hadrian, 117–138

Antoninus Pius, 138–161

Marcus Aurelius, 161–180

Lucius Verus, co-emperor with Marcus Aurelius 161–169

Commodus, co-emperor with Marcus Aurelius 178–180, sole emperor to 193

Pertinax, 193

Didius Julianus, 193

Septimius Severus, 193–211

Vespasian, 69–79

Augustus, 27 B.C.E.– 14 C.E.

II

MONUMENTS TO POWER

BUT WHEN IT COMES TO PUBLIC BUILDING,
YOU DO IT ON A GRAND SCALE.
—PLINY THE YOUNGER, *PANEGYRIC*
(PRAISING THE EMPEROR TRAJAN)

opposite:
A temple built in what is now southern France during the reign of Augustus

From the time of Augustus—who made a famous declaration that he had found Rome a city of brick and left it a city of marble—nearly every emperor sponsored impressive building projects. Augustus himself had eighty-two temples restored in a single year. That was just the tip of the iceberg. Along with members of his family and court, the *princeps* gave the city of Rome countless other new and renovated structures, from government buildings to bathhouses and theaters, along with bridges, aqueducts, and roads. It was not just Rome that benefitted from the emperors' construction programs—the rest of Italy, and the provinces, too, received aqueducts, roads, and impressive buildings and monuments of many kinds.

PALACES AND PLEASURE GARDENS

Augustus preferred to live fairly simply, or at least no more luxuriously than other upper-class Romans. Since he did not want to be seen as a king, he did not live in a palace but in a regular house. It was not especially elegant—marble was used nowhere in the house, nor were there any mosaic floors. There were, however, wall paintings, which were common in all upper-class Roman homes. And at his summer house on the island of Capri, he displayed his collections of fossils and ancient weapons.

Few of the emperors who came after Augustus shared his simple tastes. Tiberius built an imperial residence on Rome's Palatine Hill; it is from *Palatine* that we get the word "palace." Many later emperors lived in the palace built for Domitian on top of the Palatine (completed in 92). Everything about Domitian's palace was designed to impress people with the emperor's might. The walls of the entryway were ninety-eight feet high, the audience hall or throne room was gigantic, and the dining room used for state banquets was almost as large. These rooms were decorated with huge statues, rich wall paintings, and marble (in thin sheets on both walls and floors) in a wide range of colors, imported from all over the empire. The private apartments, where the imperial family lived, were just as splendid. Domitian's palace also featured a curved, two-story covered walkway along the south side of the building; four courtyards (one with a fountain surrounded by an octagonal maze); and a huge sunken garden in the shape of a racetrack.

Nearly every emperor also had several residences outside the city of Rome—villas in the countryside, summer houses by the sea. The most famous and elaborate of all these retreats was the emperor Hadrian's villa in Tivoli, about fifteen miles east of Rome.

A portion of the artistic landscaping at the emperor Hadrian's villa in Tivoli

Hadrian, who ruled from 117 to 138, was an amateur architect and designed much of the villa himself. It took ten years to construct the buildings and landscape the grounds. When the complex was finished, it was nearly one-tenth the size of the city of Rome. Along with a palace, the estate included temples, bathhouses, guesthouses, banquet halls, two libraries, a theater, a swimming pool, an art gallery, and acres and acres of gardens. There were quarters for numerous servants and guards, underground service passages, and kitchens where food could be prepared for hundreds of people at once. The crown jewel of Tivoli was the emperor's personal retreat, an elegant house on a small island surrounded by a canal, which was in turn encircled by columns and statues; the whole retreat was enclosed by a high circular wall. The only way to the island was across a single bridge, which the emperor could even remove when he especially wanted to be left alone.

BUILDING TO PLEASE THE PEOPLE

Hadrian, like most emperors, did not build just for his own pleasure. He traveled throughout the empire, visiting thirty-eight of the

The Pantheon has been turned into a Christian church, but in most ways it looks the same today as it did during the reign of Hadrian.

empire's forty-four provinces. The *Augustan Histories** tell us that "in almost every city he constructed some building." In Rome itself Hadrian restored many monuments and rebuilt the Pantheon, a temple dedicated to all the gods. He may have taken part in the groundbreaking design of the Pantheon's lofty concrete dome, which was crowned by a circular opening, thirty feet across, that allowed sunlight to fill the temple's interior.

Emperors restored and built temples to beautify the empire and to glorify Rome (represented by the gods of the state)—and to show off their magnificence and generosity. Good public relations was one of the main reasons that emperors also sponsored the building of bathhouses, not only in Rome but in cities throughout the empire. Indoor plumbing was a rarity in the ancient world—it might be available in palaces and mansions, but that was it. To get clean, the majority of people in the empire's cities had to rely on the public baths. Along with bathing facilities, the great baths constructed by various emperors also offered swimming pools, gymnasiums, snack shops, libraries, meeting rooms, and pleasure gardens. They were all-purpose fitness and social centers, and Roman city dwellers were grateful to the emperors for providing them. From time to time emperors even paid all bathers' admission fees for a day, a week, or even a month.

*Also called *Historia Augusta* or *Writers of Augustan History,* this was a late fourth-century collection of biographies of Roman emperors.

A nineteenth-century artist made this painting of the ruins of a pool in a bathing complex in Roman Britain.

The public baths were places where people of different social classes mingled, and so were the amphitheaters. These huge structures were the scenes of open-air spectacles or entertainments that were held on holidays and other special occasions. One of the most famous buildings in the world is the Colosseum, the amphitheater begun in Rome by the emperor Vespasian. With terraced seating for more than 50,000 spectators, it was dedicated in 80 C.E. by Vespasian's son and successor, Titus. To celebrate the opening of the amphitheater, Titus sponsored one hundred days of gladiator combats and wild-animal fights.

Emperors also sponsored—and attended—chariot races in Rome's ancient racetrack, the Circus Maximus. Free spectacles and entertainments helped keep the city's people content by getting them out of their cramped apartments and distracting them from their problems. In the amphitheater, the circus, and the theater, the common people also had a chance to see their emperor and even, within certain limits, to express their honest opinions about various issues. It was worth an emperor's while to appear generous and

A Roman mosaic depicts a group of musicians entertaining the public.

accessible to the people, who might otherwise riot. As the teacher and orator Fronto wrote of the emperor Trajan,

> Because of his shrewd understanding . . . , the emperor gave his attention even to actors and other performers on stage or on the race track or in the arena, since he knew that the Roman people are held in control principally by two things— free grain and shows—that political support depends as much on the entertainments as on matters of serious import, that . . . neglect of the entertainments brings damaging unpopularity, . . . [and that] the shows placate everyone.

Along with understanding the importance of keeping the people of Rome entertained, Trajan enthusiastically promoted public works projects. He was responsible for paving many roads and building bridges throughout Italy. He had new harbor facilities constructed at Ostia, Rome's seaport. In the city of Rome itself he built an aqueduct (for bringing fresh water down from the mountains), an amphitheater especially for mock sea battles, a public

❧ THE EMPEROR'S IMAGE ❧

Thanks to television, newspapers, magazines, and the Internet, our leaders are familiar faces to us. The Roman emperors also wanted their faces to be familiar to the people they governed, but they had no mass media to rely on. They had to find other means, one of which was sculpture. Every emperor had himself portrayed in marble (and sometimes in bronze)—in full-length statues, in portrait busts, in reliefs carved on buildings and monuments. Statues and busts were sent out to all parts of the empire. A single emperor's statues might portray him in a variety of ways, some of them chosen to suit specific parts of the empire: the great conqueror, the divine ruler, the philosophical thinker, the bearer of the burdens of government.

Money made the emperors' faces even more familiar to the people of the empire, for every emperor issued coins with his portrait on them. On one side of the coin the emperor was seen in profile, often with an inscription giving some or all of his titles (emperors had so many titles that they usually had to be abbreviated). The other side of the coin gave the emperor the opportunity to express a message to the people. The design might include a deity that was important to the emperor or a personification of a particular virtue or quality, such as Victory or Discipline. Other designs on coins referred in words or pictures to specific achievements, such as conquests and building programs. Some emperors used their coins to really get their message across: some of Hadrian's coins, for instance, refer to him as "the enricher of the world."

Augustus, with the words *father of the country*, on a gold coin

bath, and a multistory semicircular marketplace with room for around 170 shops, storehouses, and offices. Trajan's Market was designed by the emperor's favorite architect, Apollodorus of Damascus—one of the most admired architects in the ancient world. Apollodorus also created Trajan's Forum, the largest and grandest public meeting place in Rome, beautifully ornamented with gilded statues and marble in many colors.

EMBLEMS OF IMPERIAL MIGHT

The achievements of emperors were often honored by special monuments, such as triumphal arches. Built of stone, these imposing structures usually featured sculpted reliefs that celebrated an emperor's military victories. Some emperors had columns erected to honor their conquests. The most famous of these is Trajan's Column, which is still standing on its original site in Trajan's Forum (in ancient times, there was a library on either side of the column). One hundred feet tall, it was made from twenty huge blocks of marble and originally had a statue of the emperor on top. The entire surface was covered with reliefs illustrating Trajan's conquest of Dacia (modern Romania). This visual record begins at the bottom of the column and spirals upward in twenty-three bands of sculpted pictures that can be "read" almost like a wordless comic strip.

A different kind of military monument was built by Trajan's successor, Hadrian. On a visit to the province

Scenes of conquest cover every inch of Trajan's Column.

of Britain in 122, the emperor ordered the building of a stone wall across what is now northern England to protect the Roman territory south of the wall from raids by tribes living in what is now Scotland. The wall was about seventy-six miles long, eight to ten feet thick, and took nearly ten years to build. It was fortified by lookout towers and milecastles, small forts roughly a mile apart. Hadrian's successor, Antoninus Pius, pushed Roman rule northward and had a thirty-six-mile-long earthen wall built at the new boundary. After about ten years, though, the Antonine Wall was abandoned, and Hadrian's Wall once more marked the northernmost limit of the Roman Empire.

opposite: Trajan's column, today crowned with a statue of a Christian saint. The inside of the column is hollow; a spiral staircase with 185 marble steps leads up to the platform at the top.

III

THE IMPERIAL COURT

HIS FRIENDS HE ENRICHED GREATLY, EVEN THOUGH THEY DID NOT
ASK IT, WHILE TO THOSE WHO DID ASK, HE REFUSED NOTHING.
AND YET HE WAS ALWAYS READY TO LISTEN
TO WHISPERS ABOUT HIS FRIENDS.
—AUGUSTAN HISTORIES, LIFE OF HADRIAN

opposite:
The emperor Vespasian (right) greets his son Domitian (center), who is attended by a courtier. The figures behind them represent the geniuses, or spirits, of the Senate and the Roman people.

The emperor's court was wherever he was. Some emperors, such as Antoninus Pius, rarely left the city of Rome. Marcus Aurelius, on the other hand, spent five years of his reign in military camps along the Danube River, waging war against Germanic tribes that threatened the empire's borders. Then there was Hadrian, whose travels throughout the empire occupied a total of twelve years of his twenty-one-year reign.

In general, whether an emperor was at home in the palace, out leading the army, or visiting the provinces, he continued to mind the empire's business. He was the supreme judge in all legal cases involving Roman citizens—the final court of appeal. Foreign policy was his responsibility, and he met with ambassadors to discuss

border issues, trade agreements, and the like. Much of his time was spent on correspondence, for he had to supervise and advise provincial governors and other officials all over the empire. And of course, he was commander-in-chief of the military. Naturally, the emperor's court was filled with men of many ranks who assisted him in his various duties.

THE EMPEROR'S FRIENDS

The emperor generally had an informal council made up of men whom he knew well and trusted. Such men did not usually live at court but were summoned when the emperor wanted to discuss important issues and decisions with them. Because of their experience and good judgment, he could turn to them for reliable advice. These friends and supporters were most often senators, but sometimes they belonged to the next highest Roman rank, the *equites,* or equestrians. An important member of Augustus's court, for example, was the equestrian Maecenas. He was also a well-known patron of literature, and through him some of Rome's greatest poets became part of the emperor's circle.

Writers in fact belonged to the courts of a number of emperors. At the beginning of Nero's reign, one of his top advisers was the playwright and philosopher Seneca the Younger. Later Nero chose the novelist Petronius as, in the words of Tacitus, "one of his few intimate associates, as a critic in matters of taste, while the emperor thought nothing charming or elegant in luxury unless Petronius had expressed to him his approval of it." Suetonius, who wrote biographies of emperors and other illustrious men, was chief librarian and palace secretary to Trajan. He continued in this position for a time under Hadrian, but after a few years he was

⁓ THE PRINCEPS AND THE POETS ⟊

Augustus's good friend Maecenas loved poetry. He was an amateur poet himself, but his real gift was in recognizing and encouraging the talent of others. He gave generous financial support to such men and even brought them to the emperor's attention. Virgil, Horace, and Propertius—three of Rome's greatest poets—were all patronized by Maecenas and Augustus.

Virgil with two Muses

Maecenas suggested to each of these three that they write an epic celebrating the *princeps*'s achievements. Propertius responded with a witty poem in which he listed the deeds of Augustus that he would have included in an epic if he had been able to compose such a long, heroic poem—but after all, he concluded, he was really best at writing love poetry. Horace had also declared that he was not an epic poet, but he did write a number of shorter poems that praised Augustus. Virgil, however, early on promised that someday he would indeed write an epic. When he did, he produced one of the finest works of Latin literature, the *Aeneid*. And although the subject of the poem was Augustus's legendary heroic ancestor Aeneas, and not the *princeps* himself, Virgil still managed to glorify Augustus in a way that satisfied everyone.

Then there was Ovid, Rome's most popular poet during the reign of Augustus. Ovid had little or no contact with the court, yet the emperor couldn't help but notice him. Ovid was witty and irreverent, and he wrote many poems that poked fun at or flaunted the strict, old-fashioned values that Augustus promoted. The emperor was not amused. Even though Ovid ended his great, epic-length mythological poem *Metamorphoses* with Julius Caesar's transformation into a god, Augustus must have felt that most of Ovid's poetry was extremely immoral. Eventually the emperor sent him into exile, where he spent the rest of his life because of, as Ovid himself said, "a poem and a mistake."

⊱ OVID ON LOVE ⊰

Ovid's long poem *The Art of Love* is full of sly and witty advice about how to carry on a secret romance. In this selection, the poet suggests ways to make the most of a visit to the racetrack.

Don't neglect the horse races if you're looking for a place to meet your girlfriend. A circus crowded with people offers many advantages. You don't have to use a secret sign language here or be content with a slight nod to acknowledge one another's presence. Sit right next to your girlfriend—no one will stop you— and squeeze up beside her as closely as possible. It's really easy to do. The narrowness of each seating space forces you to squeeze together; in fact the rules for seating compel you to touch her!

Conversation should begin with no problem; just start out with the same comments that everyone else is making. Be sure to ask with great interest which horses are running and then immediately cheer for the same one, whichever it is, that she cheers for. . . .

Take advantage of every opportunity. If her skirt is trailing too far along the ground, pick up the edge of it and carefully lift the soiled part off the dust. At once you'll receive a reward for your careful concern; you'll be able to look at her legs, and she won't mind.

In addition, turn to whoever is sitting behind her and ask him not to jab her in the back with his knees. These little touches win over simple female hearts. Many men have found it useful to bring along a cushion which they can offer. It's also helpful to fan her with the racing program and to give her a stool for her dainty feet. Yes, the circus provides many opportunities for initiating a love affair.

dismissed for being disrespectful to the empress. Among Hadrian's friends and courtiers were philosophers, musicians, poets, mathematicians, and others. Galen, a man of many talents, served the emperors Marcus Aurelius, Commodus, and Septimius Severus as imperial physician. Galen also wrote works on philosophy, literature, grammar and, especially, medicine—in fact, his medical writings went on to become the standard textbooks for doctors throughout medieval Europe.

A Roman copy of the head of an ancient Greek writer. Roman emperors valued writers and philosophers as well as men of action.

Naturally, men of action often played a prominent role at court. For example, Augustus's closest friend and adviser was Marcus Agrippa, a skilled general. He was born a plebeian, or commoner, but through his own skill and intelligence rose to great influence. He supported and fought for Augustus during the civil wars, and afterward held many important government posts. He also founded the city of Cologne, Germany, as a settlement for retiring soldiers, and sponsored a number of important building projects in Rome. Augustus thought so much of Agrippa that he even had him marry his daughter Julia, his only child.

THE PRAETORIAN GUARD

The emperor's bodyguard played a very important role at court. Known as the Praetorian Guard, for most of the first two centuries of the empire it numbered around five thousand men. Praetorian soldiers took turns at guard duty in the imperial palace (receiving the watchword from the emperor himself) and protected the emperor wherever he went. If the emperor went to war, usually the

The Praetorian Guard not only protected the emperor at court, but also accompanied him in battle.

whole Praetorian Guard accompanied him—they were an elite fighting force as well as a bodyguard.

Unlike soldiers in the legions, who were recruited from all over the Roman world, nearly all the Praetorians came from Italy. From the reign of Tiberius on, they were stationed in a camp on the northeast edge of Rome. Each member of the guard was required to serve for twelve years (later increased to sixteen). The Praetorians were the highest paid soldiers in the empire, and they often received bonus payments from the emperors. Their special uniforms—with shining breastplates, plumed helmets, and oval shields—also set them apart from ordinary Roman soldiers.

The imperial bodyguard was commanded by an officer called the Praetorian prefect. He was chosen by the emperor from among the equestrians—this was one of the two top positions that men from that class could fill. (The other top post for *equites* was governor of Egypt, also appointed by the emperor.) Many ambitious equestrians strove for the emperor's recognition in the hope of someday becoming Praetorian prefect. A man who reached this goal could enjoy immense power and influence. For instance, Tiberius's Praetorian prefect Sejanus virtually ruled the empire for five years while the emperor lived in semi-retirement on the island of Capri.

The Praetorian Guard sometimes was more interested in protecting its own interests than in protecting an emperor. The

A CRAFTY COURTIER

Some emperors could be easily swayed or deceived by the flattery and cunning of their courtiers. Tiberius placed perfect trust in his energetic and efficient Praetorian prefect, Sejanus, honoring him by making him a senator and a consul. The emperor became so reliant on Sejanus that he referred to him as "my partner in toil." But, as the historian Tacitus described him, Sejanus was not the loyal, upright subject he appeared to be:

> . . . he won the heart of Tiberius so effectually by various artifices that the emperor, ever dark and mysterious towards others, was with Sejanus alone careless and freespoken. . . . He had a body which could endure hardships, and a daring spirit. He was one who screened himself, while he was attacking others; he was as cringing as he was imperious; before the world he affected humility; in his heart he lusted after supremacy, for the sake of which he was sometimes lavish and luxurious, but oftener energetic and watchful, qualities quite as mischievous when hypocritically assumed for the attainment of sovereignty.

Eventually Sejanus's deeds caught up with him. He had been responsible for murdering or exiling several members of the imperial family, including the men who were most likely to succeed Tiberius. Although Sejanus controlled all access to the emperor, who was living in seclusion on the island of Capri, Tiberius's sister-in-law Antonia managed to get a letter to him. She warned him about the Praetorian prefect's plans to rule the empire himself, and Tiberius at last became suspicious. The emperor secretly selected a new Praetorian prefect and gave him orders to arrest and kill Sejanus, whose ambitions ended in ruin.

Praetorians might fail to support a new emperor who did not pay them a bonus at the beginning of his reign. Several emperors who abused their power were murdered by members of the guard. The Praetorian Guard could also play a role in selecting a new emperor when there was no clear successor. Most famously, after Praetorian officers assassinated Gaius Caligula, they found his uncle Claudius hiding behind a curtain in the palace. The soldiers whisked him away to the Praetorian camp and proclaimed him emperor. With their loyalty sealed by huge bribes, members of the Senate were forced to accept the Praetorians' choice and voted to give Claudius all the privileges and powers of emperor.

SLAVES AND FREEDMEN

The imperial household included hundreds of slaves. Many of them performed the physical work of cleaning the palace, maintaining the gardens, laundering the emperor's togas, and so on. There were also skilled, highly trained slaves, such as cooks, physicians, and secretaries. Entertainers, both women and men, who lived at or visited the emperor's court were generally slaves, too. Among the slaves who took care of the emperor's personal needs were masseurs, barbers, and bedroom attendants (whose duties included making the bed, emptying and cleaning the chamber pot, and laying out the emperor's clothes for the day). Female slaves also lived in the palace to perform similar tasks for the women of the emperor's family.

Slaves who did their jobs well were often rewarded with their freedom. They still owed service and loyalty to the emperor, however, and often continued in their former jobs. Much of the day-to-day work of government administration was done by the imperial household's slaves and freedmen. Many were involved in keeping records and accounts and in writing up the emperor's correspondence. Some had very specialized jobs, such as the *nomenclator,* a kind of herald whose job was to announce the name of each person who came to visit the emperor.

The emperor's personal attendants had more contact with him than almost anyone else. Naturally a closeness often developed between the emperor and these servants. He might confide in them and ask them for their advice. Because of their personal connection, these men could be quite influential, becoming close advisers of the emperor. Claudius was especially well known for relying on his freedmen and entrusting them with government matters. He especially favored his chief secretary, Narcissus, and his financial secretary, Pallas. The historian Suetonius recorded that Claudius "willingly permitted" Narcissus and Pallas to be

A slave carries a tray of food in preparation for a banquet.

honoured by a decree of the Senate . . . with huge financial rewards . . .; and he also allowed them to acquire such wealth legally and illegally that one day when he was complaining of a shortage of funds, someone answered quite wittily that he would have plenty if his two freedmen made him a partner.

IV

A MAN'S WORLD

THERE CAN BE GREAT MEN EVEN UNDER BAD EMPERORS, AND DUTY
AND DISCRETION, IF COUPLED WITH ENERGY OF CHARACTER AND A
CAREER OF ACTION, WILL BRING A MAN TO . . . GLORIOUS SUMMITS.
—TACITUS, *THE LIFE OF AGRICOLA*

Men in Rome's upper class shared a common culture and common expectations of life. Their careers revolved around the law, the army, and public office. These were leadership roles, and required men to be excellent communicators—arguing court cases, issuing orders, giving speeches, writing letters and reports. Skill in the use of language was a sign of success in the Roman world—and any man who wanted to be a success had to have that skill. Wealth was also very helpful. In the top level of society, men were expected to lay out large sums of money to fund building projects, provide entertainments, assist the poor, and the like. This helped forge strong bonds between the upper class and the common people, at least in the cities. This is one reason that

Roman society remained fairly stable during the first two centuries of the empire.

THE FIRST CITIZEN

The everyday business of the empire required the emperor to spend much of his time reading and writing letters, and composing, delivering, or listening to speeches. Some emperors were famous for multi-tasking: Augustus would dictate letters while being shaved or having his hair cut. The *Augustan Histories* remarked that Hadrian "wrote, dictated, listened, and, incredible as it seems, conversed with his friends, all at one and the same time." Emperors generally also attended meetings in the Senate house on a regular basis and sat in judgment at trials.

Of course, work did not take up all an emperor's time. Like everyone else, an emperor had to eat, and dinner was often an occasion for enjoying a banquet and entertainment. Bathing, too, occupied an important place in nearly every Roman's day. Although the palace had its own bath facilities, some emperors, such as Titus and Hadrian, were singled out for praise because they "often bathed in the public baths, even with the common crowd."

As we have already seen, emperors also mingled with "the common crowd" in the theater, amphitheater, and circus. Some of Rome's rulers were not willing to be just spectators, however. Commodus shocked the Senate and common people alike by fighting as a gladiator in the arena. Gaius Caligula was so fond of chariot racing that he gave his favorite racehorse, Incitatus, "a stall of marble, a manger of ivory, purple blankets and a collar of precious stones, . . . a house, a troop of slaves and furniture"; he even invited Incitatus

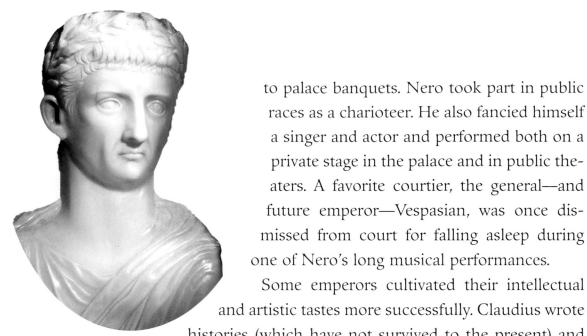

Claudius was a scholarly man, both before and after becoming emperor.

to palace banquets. Nero took part in public races as a charioteer. He also fancied himself a singer and actor and performed both on a private stage in the palace and in public theaters. A favorite courtier, the general—and future emperor—Vespasian, was once dismissed from court for falling asleep during one of Nero's long musical performances.

Some emperors cultivated their intellectual and artistic tastes more successfully. Claudius wrote histories (which have not survived to the present) and invented three new letters of the alphabet. Marcus Aurelius was a philosopher; his *Meditations,* written in Greek, is still a classic. Hadrian was the most wide-ranging of all in his interests and talents: he was said to be an expert in painting, arithmetic, geometry, and astrology; he sang, played the flute, and wrote poetry; and he enjoyed taking part in philosophical and literary debates. At the same time he was extremely fond of hunting and was skilled in the use of a wide variety of weapons.

THE LADDER OF SUCCESS

Hadrian, like a number of other emperors, began his career in the same manner as other high-born Roman males. He joined the army at the age of fifteen, then three years later was appointed to sit on a ten-judge panel that decided on matters of inheritance. After serving on this court, he received his first posting as a military tribune. This meant that he was second-in-command of a legion, working with the legate, or commander, and handling much of the legion's legal business. Hadrian was tribune of two different legions in turn (stationed first in what is now Hungary, then in what is now Bulgaria), before taking his first public office as quaestor.

Numerous quaestors served at once, playing various administrative and financial roles in the empire. They were involved in record keeping, worked in the treasury, and handled financial matters for provincial governors and generals in the field. Once a man had been quaestor, he automatically became a member of the Senate.

In the typical senator's career, the office of quaestor was followed by that of praetor. Praetors were judges in cases of civil law and also had responsibilities involving festivals and public games. An ex-praetor was eligible to be appointed as a legionary legate, a post he usually held for three or four years. After this he could spend a year as governor of one of the lesser provinces under the Senate's control. Then, if he had the emperor's favor, he would

A ROUTINE DAY FOR THE EMPEROR

Like most upper-class Romans, emperors often enjoyed a leisurely pace in their daily lives. This was true even of the emperors who took their responsibilities most seriously, such as Vespasian. The historian Suetonius describes for us Vespasian's "daily routine while emperor":

"He rose early, even while it was still dark. Then, after reading his letters and abstracts of official reports, he let in his friends, and while they chatted to him put on his shoes himself and got dressed. When he had dealt with any business that cropped up, he would find time for a drive and then a lie down. . . . After that he had a bath and then went through to dinner; it is said that he was at his most approachable and amenable at that time, so his household were eager to seize the opportunity of asking him something then."

An artist's reconstruction of the palace of the Roman governor of Britain, who had his headquarters in London

generally be put in charge of one of the emperor's provinces—but not one where more than a single legion was stationed.

The next step up the ladder was consul—as always, with the emperor's approval. Although consuls had very little power or responsibility under the emperors, most senators still found it an honor to hold the office. After a man had served as consul, the Senate might appoint him to a one-year term as governor of Africa (modern Tunisia and northwestern Libya) or Asia (today western Turkey), the greatest provinces under the Senate's control. Or the emperor could send him to govern a province with two or more legions, and he would stay in this office for as long as the emperor wished. Gnaeus Julius Agricola (father-in-law of the historian Tacitus) was governor of the province of Britain for seven or eight years, a fairly long time.

Between these various posts, many of which took him to the provinces, a man would spend periods at home in Rome, participating in the meetings of the Senate. He might also practice law, but senators were not allowed to engage in business. They could, however, invest in real estate, merchant expeditions, and similar moneymaking enterprises. Quite a few senators—among them the historians Tacitus and Dio Cassius—also devoted a good portion of their time to literature.

MANLY VIRTUES AND THE MILITARY

From the time of the early republic, noble Roman men were expected to live up to certain standards. Their highest calling was to serve the state, in both war and peace. The greatest virtues they could have, therefore, were *gravitas, pietas,* and *virtus.* These Latin words stood for concepts that were somewhat different from the meanings of the modern English words ("gravity," "piety," and "virtue") that descend from them. *Gravitas* basically meant "dignity," or "seriousness," and Roman noblemen and rulers were generally concerned to behave in as dignified a manner as possible, which would inspire the respect of others. *Pietas* referred to properly doing one's duty to parents, country, and the gods. *Virtus* comes from the word *vir,* "man," so literally means "manliness"—which to the Romans involved a combination of bravery, discipline, and self-sacrifice.

Virtus was first and foremost a military virtue. The Romans had always felt that military experience was essential for men in the upper classes. The leaders of the state had to have the ability to command, and the army was the best place to learn and practice this. Many reigning emperors made a point of giving their heirs a good taste of army life, as Trajan did with Hadrian. Not only did this help develop *virtus,* but it was the best way to earn the respect and loyalty of the legions. A man who had shared the hardships of camp life with the soldiers and led them to victory would sit all the more securely on his throne. And of course, army service in young

⌇⌇ FOR THE FATHERLAND ⌇⌇

One of the clearest expressions of what *virtus,* or manliness, meant to upper-class Romans can be found in a poem from Horace's third book of Odes. The poem is untitled in Latin, but English translators sometimes call it "Discipline." Here are some selections from it:

Let the vigorous boy learn well to bear
Lean hardship like a friend in bitter war,
And let the fearsome man on horse
With his spear harass the fierce Parthian
  force. . . .*

Virtus, never knowing disgraceful defeat,
Shines with untarnished pride and respect
And neither takes up nor lays down its power
At the pleasure of the people's changing favor.

It is sweet and fitting to die for the fatherland.
Besides, death hunts down a fleeing man
And for unwarlike youth shows no mercy
To cowardly back or bended knees.

Virtus, opening heaven to the deserving,
Gives proper guidance past forbidden things
And rises on soaring wings above the crowds
Of the vulgar and the clinging ground.

* The Parthians, whose homeland was in what is now northeastern Iran, were among Rome's "archenemies."

⌇⌇

manhood prepared the future emperor for his role as commander-in-chief.

Some emperors were more interested in military matters than others. Neither Gaius Caligula nor Nero ever led the army, and Claudius took no active military role in the invasion of Britain that he ordered. Vespasian became emperor because of his success as a general and his popularity with the troops, but after taking the throne he left active military command to his son Titus. Hadrian, on the other hand, was one of the emperors who was closely involved with the army both before and after coming to the throne. On a visit to Germany as emperor, Hadrian made a point of spending time among the legions stationed there. He improved their conditions and their discipline, largely through his own example, according to the *Augustan Histories:*

> Though more desirous of peace than of war, he kept the soldiers in training just as if war were imminent, inspired them by proofs of his own powers of endurance, actually led a soldier's life among [them] . . ., and, after the example of . . . his own adoptive father Trajan, cheerfully ate out of doors such camp-fare as bacon, cheese, and vinegar. . . . He incited others by the example of his own soldiery spirit; he would walk as much as twenty miles fully armed; he . . . generally wore the commonest clothing, would have no gold ornaments on his swordbelt or jewels on the clasp . . ., visited the sick soldiers in their quarters, selected the sites for camps, . . . banished luxuries on every hand, and, lastly, improved the soldiers' arms and equipment. . . . He made it a point to be acquainted with the soldiers and to know their numbers.

V

IMPERIAL WOMEN

THE EMPEROR REPEATEDLY ASSERTED THAT THERE MUST BE A LIMIT
TO THE HONORS PAID TO WOMEN.
—TACITUS, *ANNALS*

opposite:
A portrait of a Roman matron seemingly lost in thought

The imperial court was very much a man's world. Of course the emperor's wife and children, and often his mother and sisters, lived with him in the palace. But these women and children, and their female slaves and freedwomen servants, were far outnumbered by the male members of the imperial household. In both the imperial family and senatorial families, women's activities were extremely limited. While men were out and about conducting legal business or serving in the government, women were expected to mostly stay close to home and concern themselves with household and family matters. Roman historians rarely wrote much about women; when they did, it was usually to criticize a woman for scandalous behavior—which might mean little more than getting

involved in too many activities outside the home. Roman women were praised for virtues such as bravery, strength, loyalty, and devotion to duty only when those virtues served the men in their families.

OLD-FASHIONED FAMILY VALUES

Roman society was set up to put all power in the hands of men. The male head of the family had absolute authority over all his children, and often over grandchildren and other relatives as well. He decided whom they married and could also order them to divorce for any reason he pleased. (Under Roman law, children remained with their father after a divorce.) He could disown family members and punish them harshly for misbehavior. All the family finances were controlled by him, and his consent was necessary for most major decisions made by other family members. This *patria potestas,* or "power of the father," was especially dominant in the lives of women, who could never become the heads of families.

The law generally required that a woman always have a male guardian, normally her father, for her entire life. If he died, the courts would appoint another guardian. A woman could not handle financial, business, or legal matters without her guardian's permission and assistance. From the time of Augustus, however, the law allowed a mother of three children to be freed from guardianship.

The first emperor was very disturbed by recent trends in Roman society. People were often staying unmarried, or marrying later in life, or not having children when they did marry, especially in the upper class. Augustus wanted to change this situation, to strengthen the family and keep it at the center of society. He created laws that rewarded people for having three or more children, punished them (by reducing their right to inherit property) for remaining unmarried or childless, and required women to remarry after being widowed or divorced. These laws also tried to control other aspects of women's and men's private lives.

In spite of the legislation, the birth rate among the upper class does not seem to have increased. This is partly because pregnancy and childbirth were extremely risky for women in ancient times. Even with the best health care, many diseases and problems were not preventable, and there were few medical techniques that could help a woman if something went wrong during pregnancy or birth. Miscarriages were common and many women—and their babies— died from childbirth complications. Very often, parents who dearly wanted to have many children just were not able to. Among such parents was Augustus himself. His only child was his daughter, Julia, from his second marriage.

POWER BEHIND THE THRONE

Augustus divorced his second wife to marry Livia, who belonged to one of Rome's oldest and most influential noble families. She was already married and was pregnant with her second child, but the emperor ordered her husband to divorce her. After that, according to Suetonius, Livia was "the one woman he truly loved until his death." Augustus certainly valued her, trusting her to meet with ambassadors when he was busy with other matters. He not only asked her for advice on a regular basis but also took notes on what she said so that he could study it later. When Livia's son Tiberius succeeded to the throne, Livia expected her influence to continue. The new emperor, however, felt that his mother was

Livia and her son Tiberius as a child

A DAUGHTER RULED BY HER FATHER

Augustus was an old-fashioned father and insisted that his daughter, Julia, spend her time spinning and weaving like the virtuous Roman women of earlier days. (Julia and her stepmother made most of the emperor's clothes themselves.) She was strictly supervised, seldom allowed to go out, and was not allowed to have any boyfriends.

Like many upper-class Roman daughters, Julia was at the mercy of her father's ambitions. At the age of fourteen, Augustus had her marry his nephew Marcellus, who was in his late teens at the time. The young man died two years later, in 23 B.C.E., leaving no children behind. Augustus was determined that Julia bear children who could succeed him, so in 21 B.C.E. he married her to his friend Agrippa—after making Agrippa divorce the wife he already had. Agrippa was twenty-five years older than Julia, but they had five children together, and Augustus adopted

A young woman picking spring flowers

the two oldest boys to be his heirs.

When Agrippa died in 12 B.C.E., the emperor worried about who would be his heirs' guardian if he should die. He forced his stepson Tiberius to divorce his wife, whom he loved deeply, and early in the next year Julia was married to him. Tiberius never came to love—or even like—Julia, and life at court was unpleasant for him in other ways. With Augustus's permission, he left Rome and Julia (five years after their wedding) to live on the Greek island of Rhodes.

Julia took the opportunity to rebel against her strict upbringing and her arranged marriages. Roman authors later exaggerated her misconduct, but she certainly did not uphold her father's ideas about proper moral behavior for women. In 2 B.C.E., after denouncing her to the entire Senate, Augustus condemned Julia to exile. She died in despair fifteen years later, not long after her father's death.

constantly interfering with affairs that shouldn't concern her, and he resented her for it. For good or ill, she remained a powerful force at court until her death at the unusually ripe old age of eighty-six.

Livia set a pattern for many of the imperial women of the first century. Proud of their descent from Augustus or from ancient noble families, a number of them were strong-willed and eager to play a part in ruling the empire. Their actions were always unofficial, of course, since no Roman woman could hold office or even vote. But simply through their closeness to the emperor, they could achieve great influence.

Gaius Caligula, for example, was an extremely unstable man, but his sister Drusilla was able to keep him from getting too out of hand until her death in the second year of his reign. His youngest sister, Agrippina, eventually married his successor, Claudius. She was able to take on some official duties (scandalizing many Romans), appearing in civic ceremonies and publicly receiving ambassadors in a way that even Livia had not done. Agrippina also schemed to have her son, Nero, made the emperor's heir. She was willing to use any means necessary—including having Claudius poisoned when she feared he would put a stop to her plans.

On Nero's first day as emperor, the password he gave to the Praetorian Guard was "best of mothers." His mother was the dominant influence on his life, and at first he was devoted to her. But it seemed that what she really wanted was to rule the empire through her son. Before long Nero was fed up with her interference and refused to let her live in the palace any longer. Then, his frustration turning to hatred, Nero arranged to have Agrippina killed. Tacitus related, "Many years before Agrippina had anticipated this end for herself. . . . For when she consulted the astrologers about Nero,

The empress Sabina often felt ignored by her husband, but she remained a devoted wife.

they replied that he would be emperor and kill his mother. 'Let him kill her,' she said, 'provided he is emperor.'"

After the reign of Nero, empresses and other women of the imperial family generally seem to have exercised their influence more quietly—and more peacefully. Titus's daughter, Julia Titi, for example, suggested to her father the nomination of a particular man for consul. Trajan's wife, Plotina, was sometimes criticized for the determination with which she arranged for Hadrian to succeed her husband. More often, though, she was praised for being a model of womanly modesty and virtue. She is known to have advised both Trajan and Hadrian in political matters, and her advice was valued.

Plotina also encouraged her husband to marry his great-niece Sabina to Hadrian. This marriage may not have been a very happy one—Hadrian complained about Sabina's moodiness—but the two worked well together as emperor and empress, if not as husband and wife. We know that Sabina accompanied Hadrian on at least some of his travels: her friend Julia Balbilla, a Greek noblewoman, inscribed a poem on the leg of an ancient Egyptian statue to commemorate the empress's visit to Egypt.

WOMEN OF WORTH AND WEALTH

Perhaps one of the happiest of all imperial marriages was that of Antoninus Pius and Annia Galeria Faustina. The emperor once said of his wife, "by heaven, I would rather live with her on Gyara [in exile] than in the palace without her." Many husbands and wives had similar feelings. Even though all upper-class Roman marriages were arranged, the spouses often grew to love and respect each other. Divorce was common and easy to obtain, and people often remarried after being widowed. But the ideal for both men and women was still felt to be lifelong marriage to one person. An upper-class husband, speaking at his wife's funeral in about 10 C.E., said, "Rare indeed are marriages of such long duration, which are ended by death, not divorce. We had the good fortune to spend forty-one years together with no unhappiness."

☙ A SENATOR'S WIFE ❧

Pliny the Younger, a senator with a successful law career and an excellent record in public service, was also a famous writer and orator. He was devoted to his young wife, Calpurnia, and praised her excellent qualities in this letter he wrote to her aunt:

My wife is very sensible and very thrifty. And she loves me, surely an indication of her virtue. She has even, because of her affection for me, taken an interest in literature. She has copies of my books, she reads them over and over again, and even learns them by heart. What anxiety she feels when I am going to plead a case in court, what great relief when I have finished! She even stations slaves to report to her on the approval and the applause I receive, and on what verdict I obtain in the case. And whenever I give a recitation, she sits nearby, concealed behind a curtain, and listens very eagerly to the praise I win. She even sets my poems to music and sings them, to the accompaniment of a lyre. No musician has taught her, but love itself, the best of instructors.

·VI·

CHILDREN OF THE EMPIRE

HE PASSED HIS BOYHOOD AND YOUTH IN THE CULTIVATION
OF EVERY WORTHY ATTAINMENT.
—TACITUS, *THE LIFE OF AGRICOLA*

All Roman babies were born at home. Fathers generally preferred sons to daughters, but wealthy families (who did not have to worry about having too many mouths to feed) were usually overjoyed by the birth of any healthy child. Nine days after birth, a ceremony of purification was held to protect the baby from evil. Then the child was formally named and given a *bulla,* a good luck charm often made of gold. Occasionally parents went even further to try to guarantee good fortune for their newborn. Gaius Caligula, for instance, carried his baby daughter Julia Drusilla to every temple of every goddess in Rome so that she would be blessed by them all.

Sometimes, even when a baby was born healthy, the mother did not survive childbirth. The father would then hire a wetnurse to

opposite:
A baby boy with
his pet goose,
carved in marble

breastfeed the baby. Some healthy Roman mothers felt that breast-feeding was beneath their dignity, and so their children, too, might be nurtured by wetnurses. Nurses were usually slaves or freed-women. The first-century orator Quintilian recommended, "Above all, make sure that the infant's nurse speaks correctly. . . . Of course, she should without doubt be chosen on the basis of good moral character, but make sure that she speaks correctly as well. The child will hear his nurse first, and will learn to speak by imitating her words." A nurse often continued to care for a child after he or she was weaned, with lasting affection forming between the two.

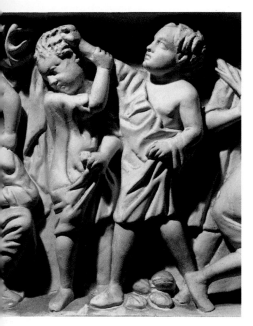

One of a *paedagogus's* duties was to protect his young charge—which included keeping the child out of fights like this one.

Another important person in a young child's life, especially a boy's, was the *paedagogus,* also a slave. His job was to rock the cradle and babysit, then to play with the child, take him on outings, and teach him table manners and perhaps the beginnings of reading and writing. As a boy grew still older, the *paedagogus* became a protector who escorted him to and from school, the baths, the theater, and elsewhere, shielding him from any immoral influences on the way. Many boys grew up feeling the same affection for their *paedagogi* as for their nurses. As an expression of gratitude, these slaves often received their freedom when their charges became adults.

PLAYTIME AND SCHOOL DAYS

Upper-class Roman children had more time for play than poorer children, who often had to start helping their families at a very young age. And of course, being wealthy, children of imperial and senatorial families had their choice of many toys. Among others, there were dolls, balls, tops, marbles, boardgames, hobbyhorses, model chariots, and (though only for boys) wooden swords and shields. Some boys had miniature chariots that they could ride in, pulled by a goat.

ROMAN CHECKERS
A GAME TO PLAY TODAY

The Roman *ludus calculi,* or "game of stones," was popular with people of all ages. It's a little like checkers and is still fun today. The Romans played it with stones or glass markers, and their board was generally not checkered but just had a grid of lines marked on it. However, a regular checkerboard will work just fine. To start, each player needs thirty-five checkers. Or you can use small, smooth stones or some other kind of markers instead, so long as you have two different colors (in the instructions below, we'll assume they're black and red).

Black goes first. The players take turns placing their markers on the board, one at a time. There is no jumping or other movement of a marker once it's been placed. The goal is to be the first person to get five markers in a row. They can be in a horizontal, vertical, or diagonal line. The challenge is that you have to block the other player from completing his or her line at the same time you're working on yours.

Unless you have no other possible move, you are not allowed to make a "double open-ended three" in any direction, for example:

Otherwise you can place your markers in any way you like. If neither player gets five in a row and all the squares are filled, the game is a draw. Time to play again!

A boy reciting his lessons to his tutor. This image comes from the child's sarcophagus, or stone coffin; he died at the age of ten.

Roman children began learning from their parents at an early age. Parents were encouraged to make learning fun and not to push too hard. They usually taught the alphabet, the basics of reading, and perhaps some simple math. What was most important, though, was for the parents to give their children a moral education. They might do this by reading or telling stories about great Roman heroes of the past, so that children could learn from these famous examples of *gravitas, pietas,* and *virtus.*

Formal education typically began at about age seven. Children of very wealthy families were generally taught at home by tutors. Augustus hired a famous teacher to move into the palace and educate his grandsons. Many other emperors had palace schools where they employed the best tutors to instruct children of the imperial family. Children of favored senators and others might also be invited to the imperial school. Claudius, for instance, rewarded Vespasian for his military service in the invasion of Britain by giving his son Titus a court education.

The most important part of an upper-class boy's formal education was training in Latin and Greek, literature, and public speaking. Math was of next importance, but science was studied little, if at all. Many boys also studied philosophy, but the general opinion was that it was not proper for high-ranking Romans to be too interested in philosophy. As a boy, Hadrian was so fond of Greek literature and Greek philosophy that people nicknamed him Greekling. Hadrian didn't seem to mind, and continued to love all things Greek for the rest of his life. Many upper-class Roman boys, in fact, finished their formal education with a tour of Greece, where they could study with some of the best orators to be found.

Roman girls received much less education than boys. They did learn Latin and literature, perhaps Greek, and probably a little math. Training in public speaking was considered unnecessary, however; household skills were much more important. While the daughters of wealthy families would never need to cook or clean for themselves, they would have to supervise the slaves who did such work, and they usually were expected to know how to spin and weave.

BECOMING AN ADULT

Childhood ended very early for upper-class girls, who could (and often did) marry as young as twelve. Their husbands were usually in at least their mid-twenties, but they might be quite a bit older, perhaps even in their fifties, having already been married once or twice. The marriage was often arranged for financial or political

❧ A TURBULENT CHILDHOOD ❧

Upper-class children grew up in a variety of settings and could experience huge ups and downs. As a young child, Gaius Caligula, along with his mother and siblings, lived in an army camp while his father was commanding the legions stationed in Germany. His parents often dressed him up in a miniature army uniform, including the tough sandals called *caligae*. Because of this the soldiers, who were fond of him, nicknamed him Caligula. Afterward he went with his parents to his father's next posting, in Syria, but there his father died (perhaps poisoned).

When Gaius was fifteen his second-oldest brother was arrested for treason. Two years later his mother and oldest brother were sent into exile because the emperor Tiberius suspected them of plotting against him. By the time Gaius was twenty-one, all three were dead. Meanwhile, he briefly lived with his grandmother, then was summoned to join the emperor on Capri, where he stayed until he himself became emperor.

reasons, and the girl's feelings might not be taken into account at all. It was her duty, and part of the virtue of *pietas,* to gladly accept her father's choice of a husband.

An older husband often took it on himself to finish his young wife's education, perhaps polishing her manners and her appreciation of literature. For example, Pliny had a friend who, he wrote, "has recently read me some letters which he said were written by his wife. . . . Whether they are really his wife's, as he says, or his own . . . one can only admire him either for what he writes, or the way he has cultivated and refined the taste of the girl he married."

Boys spent their teen years finishing their education, especially honing their public-speaking skills. Between the ages of fifteen and eighteen, it was time for the coming-of-age ceremony. An upper-class boy in Rome first went to the household shrine of his family's protector deities. There he left his *bulla* and his purple-bordered toga, the garment of childhood. This was replaced with the pure white toga of manhood. Then his family and friends accompanied him to the Forum, where he was formally proclaimed a citizen. After a visit to the city's most important temple, the rest of the day was spent feasting and celebrating. Once a boy came of age, he could begin his career in the military and government.

~VII~

PRIVILEGE AND PERIL

I ADMIRE HIM ALL THE MORE FOR THIS VERY REASON, THAT AMID
UNUSUAL AND EXTRAORDINARY DIFFICULTIES HE BOTH
SURVIVED HIMSELF AND PRESERVED THE EMPIRE.
—DIO CASSIUS ON EMPEROR MARCUS AURELIUS

opposite:
This artist's reconstruction of part of a Roman villa shows the luxury and splendor that surrounded the patricians.

The senatorial families and the imperial court made up a small percentage of the people of ancient Rome. This minority controlled most of the empire's wealth. As we have seen, the patricians frequently used their wealth for the public good, from building temples and aqueducts to contributing funds to feed the poor. Like the rich and powerful of every time and place, they also spent their money on luxuries and entertainments. Those at the highest levels of power certainly enjoyed equally high privileges. At the same time, although they were secure from hunger and want, they were, like everyone else, vulnerable to illnesses and injuries. And when it came to struggles for power or the fears and whims of an unstable emperor, the patricians might pay a high price for living at the top of society.

THE BENEFITS OF GOOD LIVING

Wealthy Romans had perhaps the highest standard of living in the ancient world. They dressed in clothes of silk, linen, or the finest wool, often dyed in jewellike colors. Women wore perfume, cosmetics, and plenty of jewelry; both sexes might dye their hair or wear wigs. Upper-class homes were spacious and beautifully decorated—and most well-off families had one or more country villas in addition to their house in Rome.

With all their needs attended to by slaves, Romans at this level of society had plenty of leisure time. Literary senators liked to hold and attend recitations, where poems, histories, and other works were recited, or read aloud, often by the author himself. Others enjoyed going to gladiatorial combats, wild-animal fights, and chariot races. Everyone liked to have a good afternoon bath and massage, perhaps with an exercise session or ball game first.

After bathtime came dinnertime, the highlight of many a Roman's day. Although Augustus was well-known for preferring plain food such as bread, herring, cheese, and green figs, very few of his successors—or other wealthy Romans—were content with such simple meals. Banquets were held frequently, with numerous courses served on silver dishes. Along with good conversation, there was usually entertainment of some kind: plays, poetry readings, music, acrobats, or dancers. Sometimes banqueters enjoyed games or a little gambling. Writing of Augustus, Suetonius related that "at some dinner parties he would auction tickets for prizes of most unequal value, and paintings with their faces turned to the wall, for which every guest present was expected to bid blindly, taking his chance like the rest: he might either pick up most satisfactory bargains, or throw away his money."

EAT LIKE AN EMPEROR

Upper-class Romans often served elaborate dinners in their gardens. The guests reclined, leaning on their left elbows, on couches around a central table. People used knives for cutting meat and spoons for eating soup, but otherwise ate with their fingers. Dinnertime in ancient Rome came in late afternoon—and if dinner was a banquet, it could last for hours.

There were three parts to each dinner, and each could have many dishes. First came appetizers, then the main course, and finally dessert. Common appetizers were egg dishes, raw vegetables, and fish. The main course was meats and cooked vegetables. This was where the greatest variety and most elaborate preparation could come in. Dessert was generally fruit and pastries. The usual drink was wine, sometimes flavored with spices.

Emperors and wealthy Romans ate many exotic foods, such as sea urchins, roasted peacocks, and flamingoes' tongues. They had large staffs of well-trained slaves to cook and serve their meals. Today it would be difficult for most people to prepare a whole banquet fit for an emperor. But here is a version of a vegetable recipe that was created for the emperor Commodus:

INGREDIENTS:
- 1 lb. fresh green beans
- 1 tsp. ground pepper
- 1/2 tsp. ground celery seed
- a pinch of ground aniseed
- 2 tsp. chopped onions
- 1 cup chicken stock
- 3 well-beaten egg yolks

- Cook the beans in 1/2 cup water for just a few minutes. Drain the beans but save the water.
- For the sauce: in a bowl, mix together the pepper, celery seed, and aniseed. Add one tablespoon of the water the beans were cooked in. Stir in the onions, chicken stock, and egg yolks.
- Put the beans in a casserole. Pour the sauce over the beans.
- Bake at 325° until the dish is firm.
Serve and enjoy!

To entertain the common people, their courts, and themselves, emperors frequently produced spectacles, for example flooding an arena and staging mock sea battles. One of the most lavish productions of all was Gaius Caligula's two-mile-long bridge of boats. The emperor had merchant ships line up across the Bay of Naples, and a road was built on top of them. During two days of festivities Caligula, dressed in splendid costumes, raced across the boat-bridge, first on a fast horse and then in a two-horse chariot, accompanied by the entire Praetorian Guard and all his friends in chariots. Extravaganzas like this were impressive and enjoyed by many, but they were expensive to produce, even for an emperor. Too many spectacles of this sort would cause a drain on the imperial treasury—a sure sign of trouble coming.

DANGER IN HIGH PLACES

As we have seen, just because a man was emperor did not mean that he was indestructible. Half of the first twenty Roman emperors died from old age, strokes, or illnesses such as malaria and cancer. The other half died by violence. Two committed suicide, and the rest were assassinated. The murderers were nearly always people close to the emperor: Praetorian Guardsmen, freedmen of the court, even family members.

When it came to palace plots, women could be every bit the equal of men, it seems. Two of Gaius Caligula's sisters, for example, were involved in a conspiracy to overthrow him and were sent into exile. Claudius's third wife, Messalina, schemed to marry another man and make him emperor. (We have already encountered the plotting of Claudius's fourth wife, Agrippina.) There were many rumors about women at the imperial court who poisoned possible heirs so that their own sons or favorites could succeed to the throne.

The very possibility of conspiracies afflicted some emperors severely. Tiberius retired to the island of Capri largely because he was so worried about plots against him. Toward the end of his reign, his fears led to a large number of treason trials in Rome.

ᴖ HOW TO SURVIVE LIFE'S TRIALS ᴕ

The philosopher-emperor Marcus Aurelius was a follower of the Stoic school of philosophy. Stoicism taught that people should train themselves to be ruled by reason so that they would not be troubled by worries or strong emotions; this was the way to be truly happy and live in harmony with the universe.

Such beliefs probably served Marcus Aurelius well. During his reign, the empire's border along the Danube River was continually threatened by Germanic tribes. Marcus spent years at war along the Danube frontier, while at home an epidemic of the plague raged. It was during these troubled times that he began writing his *Meditations*. In the following passage, the emperor gives some guidelines for getting through the tough times:

The first rule is, to keep an untroubled spirit; for all things must bow to Nature's law, and soon enough you must vanish into nothingness, like Hadrian and Augustus. The second is to look things in the face and know them for what they are, remembering that it is your duty to be a good man. Do without flinching what man's nature demands; say what seems to you most just—though with courtesy, modesty, and sincerity.

Executions were sometimes carried out by throwing the offenders to wild animals in the amphitheater.

Nero, too, often suspected courtiers, senators, and even family members of conspiring to overthrow him. Like Tiberius, he was sometimes right. But Nero's drastic measures to deal with conspirators and potential troublemakers—executing or exiling many senators and others, sometimes on the slimmest evidence—made him even more likely to be the victim of plots.

Events like these show how dangerous it sometimes was to be part of the circle of power. The senator and author Pliny the Younger lived through the reign of Domitian, another emperor whose tyrannical behavior and extreme insecurity resulted in sweeping executions. Pliny experienced the last four years of Domitian's rule as "a time when seven of my friends had been put to death or banished . . ., and there were certain clear indications to make me suppose a like end was awaiting me." Tacitus, who also survived this period, described "the senate-house besieged," "the senate hemmed in by armed men," numbers of ex-consuls "falling at one single massacre," and "many of Rome's noblest ladies exiles and fugitives."

Today, Nero and Domitian are also remembered for relentlessly persecuting the early Christians. These persecutions and other acts of violence and cruelty are often the main things that many people associate with the Roman emperors. We need to balance this image, however, with the memory of those emperors who governed justly and well. Their world was not perfect, and yet it has left us much that is inspiring: great works of literature, structures that have stood for two thousand years, beautiful paintings and statues, and stories of bravery, love, and devotion among people much like us.

GLOSSARY

amphitheater an oval stadium, mainly for shows involving combat or wild-animal fights

aqueduct an artificial channel to carry water from its source to a city

arena an amphitheater's central, ground-level area, where the amphitheater's shows took place

circus a long, oval stadium where chariot races were held; a racetrack

dowry money and/or goods that a woman's family gave her to take into her marriage

equites (EH-quee-tays) members of Rome's second highest class, ranking below senators. In general, they were wealthy businessmen. *Equites* literally means "knights," because in early Roman times these were the men wealthy enough to afford warhorses and equipment for fighting on horseback.

eulogy a speech given at a funeral to praise the dead person. Upperclass Romans often delivered eulogies in the Forum and then had them inscribed on marble.

forum the civic center and main meeting place of a Roman city, with government buildings, offices, shops, and temples surrounding a large open area. In Rome itself there were six fora: the ancient original Forum, and additional fora built by Julius Caesar and by the emperors Augustus, Nerva, Vespasian, and Trajan.

gladiator a professional fighter (nearly always a slave) trained for combat in the amphitheater

imperium "supreme command"—the power to command troops, interpret the law, and pass judgement (including the death sentence) on offenders

legate a man who commanded armed forces on behalf of the emperor

lyre a stringed instrument a bit like a small harp

orator a person skilled in writing and making speeches

pantomime a ballet-like performance in which dancers, accompanied by music, wordlessly acted out stories, usually from myth or legend. The performers were generally slaves and included women as well as men.

patron an upper-class Roman who gave financial support and other assistance to lower-ranking men. Patrons who were interested in literature often supported poets and other writers.

personification a deity or imaginary being that represents a thing or idea

plebeians commoners, the social class to which most Romans belonged

relief a form of sculpture in which the images project out from a flat surface

villa a country estate

FOR FURTHER READING

Amery, Heather, and Patricia Vanags. *Rome & Romans.* London: Usborne, 1997.

Corbishley, Mike. *What Do We Know about the Romans?* New York: Peter Bedrick Books, 1991.

Denti, Mario. *Journey to the Past: Imperial Rome.* Austin and New York: Raintree Steck-Vaughn, 2001.

Ganeri, Anita. *How Would You Survive as an Ancient Roman?* New York: Franklin Watts, 1995.

Hart, Avery, and Sandra Gallagher. *Ancient Rome! Exploring the Culture, People and Ideas of This Powerful Empire.* Charlotte, VT: Williamson Publishing, 2002.

Hinds, Kathryn. *The Ancient Romans.* New York: Benchmark Books, 1997.

Hodge, Susie. *Ancient Roman Art.* Chicago: Heinemann Library, 1998.

Jovinelly, Joann, and Jason Netelkos. *The Crafts and Culture of the Romans.* New York: Rosen Publishing Group, 2002.

Macdonald, Fiona. *The Roman Colosseum.* New York: Peter Bedrick Books, 1996.

———. *Women in Ancient Rome.* New York: Peter Bedrick Books, 2000.

Mann, Elizabeth. *The Roman Colosseum.* New York: Mikaya Press, 1998.

Nardo, Don. *Life in Ancient Rome.* San Diego, CA: Lucent Books, 1997.

———. *Life of a Roman Soldier.* San Diego, CA: Lucent Books, 2001.

———. *The Roman Empire.* San Diego, CA: Lucent Books, 1994.

Whittock, Martyn. *The Colosseum and the Roman Forum.* Chicago: Heinemann Library, 2003.

ONLINE INFORMATION*

Ancient Rome.

    http://www.mce.k12tn.net/ancient_rome/rome.htm

Carr, Karen E. *History for Kids: Ancient Rome.*

    http://www.historyforkids.org/learn/romans/index.htm

Goldberg, Dr. Neil. *The Rome Project.*

    http://www.dalton.org/groups/rome/index.html

Illustrated History of the Roman Empire.

    http://www.roman-empire.net/

Michael C. Carlos Museum of Emory University. *Odyssey Online: Rome.*

    http://carlos.emory.edu/ODYSSEY/ROME/homepg.html

Nova Online. *Secrets of Lost Empires: Roman Bath.*

    http://www.pbs.org/wgbh/nova/lostempires/roman

The Roman Empire in the First Century.

    http://www.pbs.org/empires/romans

Secrets of the Dead: The Great Fire of Rome.

    http://www.pbs.org/wnet/secrets/case_rome/index.html

Thayer, Bill. *Lacus Curtius: Into the Roman World.*

    http://www.ukans.edu/history/index/europe/ancient_rome/E/
    Roman/home.html

*All Internet sites were available and accurate when this book was sent to press.

BIBLIOGRAPHY

Adkins, Lesley, and Roy A. Adkins. *Handbook to Life in Ancient Rome.* New
York and Oxford: Oxford University Press, 1994.

Boardman, John, et al., editors. *The Oxford Illustrated History of the Roman
World.* Oxford and New York: Oxford University Press, 1988.

Davenport, Basil, editor. *The Portable Roman Reader.* New York: Penguin, 1979.

Editors of Time-Life Books. *Rome: Echoes of Imperial Glory.* Alexandria,
VA: Time-Life Books, 1994.

Editors of Time-Life Books. *What Life Was Like when Rome Ruled the
World: The Roman Empire 100 BC-AD 200.* Alexandria, VA: Time-
Life Books, 1997.

Edwards, John. *Roman Cookery: Elegant & Easy Recipes from History's First
Gourmet.* rev. ed. Point Roberts, WA: Hartley & Marks, 1986.

Fantham, Elaine, et al. *Women in the Classical World: Image and Text.* New
York and Oxford: Oxford University Press, 1994.

Grabsky, Phil. *I, Caesar: Ruling the Roman Empire.* London: BBC Books, 1997.

Kamm, Antony. *The Romans: An Introduction.* New York and London:
Routledge, 1995.

Mellor, Ronald, editor. *The Historians of Ancient Rome: An Anthology of the
Major Writings.* New York and London: Routledge, 1998.

Santosuosso, Antonio. *Storming the Heavens: Soldiers, Emperors, and Civilians
in the Roman Empire.* Boulder, CO: Westview Press, 2001.

Scarre, Chris. *Chronicle of the Roman Emperors: The Reign-by-Reign Record of
the Rulers of Imperial Rome.* London and New York: Thames &
Hudson, 1995.

Shelton, Jo-Ann. *As the Romans Did: A Source Book in Roman Social History.*
2nd ed. New York and Oxford: Oxford University Press, 1998.

Wells, Colin. *The Roman Empire.* 2nd ed. Cambridge, MA: Harvard
University Press, 1992.

SOURCES FOR QUOTATIONS

Chapter I

p. 1 "It became essential": Mellor, *The Historians of Ancient Rome,* p. 478.

p. 4 "Nothing . . . was done": Shelton, *As the Romans Did,* p. 229.

p. 4 "the Romans and their allies": ibid., p. 235.

p. 5 "to make levies": ibid., p. 228.

p. 7 "futility of long speeches": Boardman, *The Oxford Illustrated History of the Roman World,* p. 132.

p. 8 "even if he did": Scarre, *Chronicle of the Roman Emperors,* p. 95.

Chapter II

p. 10 "But when it comes": Scarre, *Chronicle of the Roman Emperors,* p. 97.

p. 14 "in almost every city": ibid., p. 102.

p. 16 "Because of his shrewd": Shelton, *As the Romans Did,* p. 334.

p. 17 "the enricher": Editors of Time-Life, *Rome: Echoes of Imperial Glory,* p. 81.

Chapter III

p. 20 "His friends he enriched": Mellor, *The Historians of Ancient Rome,* p. 503.

p. 22 "one of his few": ibid., p. 477.

p. 23 "a poem and a mistake": translation of *"carmen et error,"* Boardman, *The Oxford Illustrated History of the Roman World,* p. 203.

p. 24 "Don't neglect": Shelton, *As the Romans Did,* pp. 51–52.

p. 27 "my partner in toil": Tacitus, *Annals,* quoted in Wells, *The Roman Empire,* p. 105.

p. 27 "he won the heart": Mellor, *The Historians of Ancient Rome,* p. 445.

p. 29 "willingly permitted," "honoured by": Wells, *The Roman Empire,* p. 115.

Chapter IV

p. 30 "There can be great": Boardman, *The Oxford Illustrated History of the Roman World,* p. 132.

p. 31 "wrote, dictated, listened": Mellor, *The Historians of Ancient Rome,* p. 506.

p. 31 "often bathed": *Augustan Histories,* quoted in Mellor, *The Historians of Ancient Rome,* p. 504.

p. 31 "a stall of marble": Suetonius, *The Life of Gaius Caligula,* quoted in Mellor, *The Historians of Ancient Rome,* p. 389.

p. 33 "daily routine": Kamm, *The Romans,* pp. 68–69.

p. 36 "Let the vigorous": author's translation of *Odes,* Book III, Ode II. original Latin text at http://www.thelatinlibrary.com/horace/carm3.shtml

p. 37 "Though more desirous": Mellor, *The Historians of Ancient Rome,* pp. 499–500.

Chapter V

p. 38 "The emperor repeatedly": Mellor, *The Historians of Ancient Rome,* p. 424.

p. 41 "the one woman": Wells, *The Roman Empire,* p. 19.

p. 43 "best of mothers": Scarre, *Chronicle of the Roman Emperors,* p. 51.

p. 43 "Many years before": Mellor, *The Historians of Ancient Rome,* p. 470.

p. 44 "by heaven": Scarre, *Chronicle of the Roman Emperors,* p. 110.

p. 45 "Rare indeed": Shelton, *As the Romans Did,* p. 292.

p. 45 "My wife is very": ibid., p. 45.

p. 46 "your modesty": ibid., p. 292.

p. 46 "How could the desire": ibid., p. 294.

p. 47 "Ummidia Quadratilla": ibid., pp. 300–301.

Chapter VI

p. 48 "He passed his boyhood": Mellor, *The Historians of Ancient Rome,* p. 395.

p. 50 "Above all, make sure": Shelton, *As the Romans Did,* p. 32.

p. 51 Roman checkers adapted from Wladyslaw Jan Kowalski, *Roman Board Games.*

http://www.personal.psu.edu/users/w/x/wxk116/roma/rbgames.html

p. 55 "has recently read": Fantham, *Women in the Classical World,* p. 349.

Chapter VII

p. 56 "I admire him": Scarre, *Chronicle of the Roman Emperors,* p. 118.

p. 58 "at some dinner": Grabsky, *I, Caesar,* p. 74.

p. 59 Recipe adapted from Edwards, *Roman Cookery,* p. 76.

p. 61 "The first rule is": Scarre, *Chronicle of the Roman Emperors,* p. 118.

p. 62 "a time when": Kamm, *The Romans*, 83.

p. 63 "the senate-house besieged": Mellor, *The Historians of Ancient Rome,* p. 415.

INDEX

ABOUT THE AUTHOR

FOX GRADIN, CELESTIAL STUDIOS PHOTOGRAPHY

KATHRYN HINDS grew up near Rochester, New York. In college she studied music and writing, and went on to do graduate work in comparative literature and medieval studies at the City University of New York. She has written a number of books for young people, including Benchmark Books' LIFE IN THE MIDDLE AGES series and LIFE IN THE RENAISSANCE series. Kathryn now lives in Georgia's Blue Ridge Mountains with her husband, their son, two dogs, and three cats. When she is not writing, she enjoys dancing, reading, playing music, and taking walks in the woods.